Railways & Recollections 1961 Volume 2

Contents

Series Introduction

The *Recollections Series* is a growing collection of titles providing in an accessible way, a juxtapositioning of photographic illustration of a transport subject with the events, happenings and highlights of a wider sphere and calendar. This series, takes a particular year and place with the views displayed alongside a carefully selected pot-pourri of what happened in that twelve-month period. The vast majority of the images in the first few books were from the Ray Ruffelll collection, held by the publisher, but material from other sources is now being interspersed where felt necessary to maintain appropriate variety. The main criterion for inclusion in these books is for the images to be both interesting and aesthetically pleasing within a chosen theme.

The books are aimed at a more general market than mere transport aficionados or enthusiasts and the authors hope and trust that they will be sure in their aim and that you, the reader, will find much to enjoy, appreciate, enthuse about and even smile about! And it is hoped that some of your own memories are stirred along the way and that you may wish to share these with friends!

© Peter Townsend & John Stretton 2010

First published in 2010

ISBN 978 1 85794 338 2
Silver Link Publishing Ltd
The Trundle
Ringstead Road
Great Addington
Kettering
Northants NN14 4BW

Tel/Fax: 01536 330588
email: sales@nostalgiacollection.com

Website: www.nostalgiacollection.com

British Library Cataloguing in Publication Data
A catalogue record for this book is available from the British Library.

Printed and bound in Czech Republic

Frontispiece: **READING SOUTH** A cheery trio but, sadly, their names are not recorded! On 6 October, the driver and fireman of 'School's Class' No 30915 *Brighton* stand with one of their colleagues from the shed, enjoying having their portraits taken and demonstrating some of the great strength of camaraderie that existed on the railways in the days of steam. Not a regular visitor to this outpost of the Southern Region, *Brighton* obviously has steam at the ready for its next turn. Withdrawn in January 1963, its last shed was, appropriately, Brighton!

Coal shift-off shift!

Introduction

As this series has developed, your authors have had requests for specific years. Sadly, we cannot 'please all the people all the time' and some readers may have to wait longer than others. In addition, as this is a second 'bite' at 1961's cherry, when other years are yet to be investigated, one might wonder why this is so…but such has been the reaction to and popularity of Volume 1, that the decision has been taken to show more.

Many of the highlights and events of 1961 were, of course, covered in that first outing – such as the disappearance of the Farthing and the appearance of the one millionth Morris Minor (and readers are encouraged to look at Volume 1 for these) – but we have attempted to shine a light into fresh corners in this new one. Being in their teens in this year, your two authors have personal memories, many of which have remained fresh in their minds nearly four decades later! It was a world of change on our railways, with dieselisation spreading ever more widely, condemning many older loco types to the great scrapyard in the sky (as well as those on the ground!) and to a relegation of much loved types from front line rosters to more mundane duties. For example, 1961 was the last year of steam haulage for The Elizabethan non-stop express – introduced in 1953 to celebrate Her Majesty's Coronation – on the ECML between London and Edinburgh.

The world of camaraderie within the railway fraternity was suffering and being fragmented, both by the reduction in traffic and locomotive types, changes in working practices and the increasing difficulty in recruiting and retaining staff for the dirty jobs associated with steam, that were increasingly unacceptable and unappealing. New working practices increasingly disrupted teamwork and the longstanding public delight in chatting to a driver at the end of the journey was disappearing.

The demise of steam, foreshadowed in the 1955 'Modernisation Plan' to be sometime around the 1980s, would actually be in 1968, just seven years from the date of this book. Elimination would be progressive over the various regions of the UK, rather than en bloc at one fell swoop, and this year saw the early days of that process. Electrification of much of the Southern Railway/Region had begun much earlier, but steam survived there in great numbers; this was not to be the case in other regions. At the time, of course, the railway photographer was unaware of the importance of much of what he was taking – hindsight is a wonderful science and so many of the never to be repeated events were missed – but we are blessed by those who did point their cameras at what were considered 'everyday' at the time. It is only now that we can truly appreciate their legacy, as with the views in this book.

It has been another delightful experience in putting this collection together and your authors hope and trust that you will savour (and even salivate at?) the images contained within these pages. Like so many things from our past, they cannot be repeated.

Peter Townsend
Northamptonshire
March 2010

John Stretton
Gloucestershire

Right: **WATERLOO** One of the prestigious named trains out of Waterloo remaining at this time was 'The Bournemouth Belle'. Consisting of luxury Pullman coaches it ran from Sunday, 5 July 1931 until the end of steam on the Southern Region – 9 July 1967 (with a break for the war until 1947). It initially left at 10.30 a.m. to Bournemouth Central, with the return working leaving the seaside at 7.18 p.m. Later services added a stop at Southampton and ran on to Bournemouth West. At first it ran on summer Sundays but was sufficiently successful to be operating on all weekends and summer weekdays until, in 1936, it became a daily working. On Sunday, 8 October, it is seen leaving behind No 35018 *British India Line.*

Left: **WATERLOO** Some seven months earlier than above – and later in the day – No 35029 *Ellerman Lines* is viewed from the rear as it leaves on 14 March, with a 3 p.m. express bound for the West of England, with a full head of steam and safety valves lifting, and watched by the platform end 'man in a box'! A cargo and passenger shipping company that was founded in the late nineteenth century, Ellerman Lines progressively expanded, with the acquisition of smaller shipping lines, until it became one of the largest shipping firms in the world. The company suffered heavy losses to its merchant fleet during the two World Wars but recovered on each occasion; however, it faced strong competition and modernising trends in the shipping industry during the second half of the twentieth century. Its assets were subsequently sold to larger companies and the name was dropped in 2004. The loco's end was in September 1966.

Focus on London Waterloo

Left; **WATERLOO** Moments prior to the lower view on the previous page, *Ellerman Lines* is seen from a slightly more normal angle, albeit with the photographer crouching to gain this impression of pent up power. New on 30 April 1949, it first appeared in the infamous Bullied 'air-smoothed' casing, before being rebuilt in 1959 to the more usual design seen here. Prior to withdrawal in 1966, it worked out of Dover, Nine Elms and, finally, Weymouth sheds and is wearing the 70A Nine Elms shedplate in this view from 14 March. Following its retirement from BR, it was saved for the nation and is displayed at the National Railway Museum, in York. It has been sectioned to give children and adults the chance to marvel at what complex shapes are inside a locomotive, and although not everyone agrees with the cutting away of 8 tons of the locomotive in this way, there are others of the class that have been preserved in working order.

Below: **WATERLOO** Two days after the previous view, on 16 March, an older style of Southern locomotive is captured on a less prestigious working. Preparing to leave Waterloo, working as the 2.54 p.m. semi-fast service to Basingstoke, No 30798 *Sir Hectimere* quietly simmers, with steam lazily escaping from cylinders and safety valves. Designed by Maunsell, this was one of the later members of the 'King Arthur' Class, with six-wheeled tenders. Built around 1926, they were intended for Brighton line duties but were overtaken by electrification of this route in later years. No 30798 had been transferred to Salisbury two years before this view and its days ended there on 2 July 1962.

broken up for scrap. The loco was scrapped much earlier, at Cashmore's yard in Newport in January 1966.

Opposite right: **WATERLOO** The 3 p.m. 'West of England' express, seen earlier in the year on p.4 (lower), is again captured by our photographer on 11 May, this time leaving behind No 35017 *Belgian Marine*. With the safety valves lifting, the first beats of the loco beginning its journey raise the exhaust skywards. Bearing an appropriate 'London-Plymouth' headcode, the train will race westwards away from London and by late afternoon will be clearing Wiltshire and into Devon.

This page: **WATERLOO** Yet another 'Merchant Navy' – this time No 35021 *New Zealand Line* – backs out of the station on 12 May, having brought an express up from the West of England earlier in the day and now released from the buffer stops inside the massive trainshed. It will head to nearby Nine Elms shed, for coal and water and any other attention that may be needed, before being turned on the depot's turntable, ready for its next run west. New in November 1948, it's first duties were from Salisbury shed, but fairly early on its moved up to the 'smoke' and sojourn at Nine Elms. Its only other move of home was to Bournemouth on 12 June 1957, from where it saw out its days until 27 September 1965.

Opposite, far left: **WATERLOO** Another view of a 'Merchant Navy' 4-6-0 from the rear. On 16 March, No 35019 *French Lines CGT* stands in the later winter sunshine, ready to do business along the Southern Region racetrack. Known in this country by the title as worn by the locomotive, the shipping company's true identity was Compagnie Générale Transatlantique, hence the 'CGT' suffix. Although not a dominant player in the trans-Atlantic ocean liner trade, it was renowned in the early 20th century for its luxurious liners, the most notable of these being the *S.S. France*.

After turbulent inter-War years fortunes, the advent of commercial air travel in 1958 was to spell disaster for the French Line's passenger ships. Despite the launch of a new flagship *S.S. France* in 1961, passenger demand slumped as it could not match the convenience or speed of aeroplane travel. Dependent on government subsidies - finally withdrawn in 1974 - the fleet was mothballed. In 1977 the company merged with the Compagnie des Messageries Maritimes to form the Compagnie Générale Maritime; the last surviving CGT liner, the *SS France*, was beached at Alang, India in 2008 and was

1961 Sporting Highlights

Wimbledon
Celebrating its 75th Anniversary the singles winners were:
Rod Laver beats Chuck McKinley
to win Men's Singles Final:
6-3, 6-1, 6-4
Angela Mortimer beats Christine Truman
to win Women's Singles Final:
4-6, 6-4, 7-5

Phil Hill
wins the F1 Championship with Ferrari and also the Le Mans 24 Hours race

Golf
Gary Player becomes the first
non-american to win the US Masters

The FA Cup 1960/1
Tottenham Hotspur win 2 - 0 against
Leicester City

The League Cup 1960/1 (over two legs)
Aston Villa win after extra time
Rotherham 2 - 0 Aston Villa
Aston Villa 3 - 0 Rotherham (AET)

The Football League Champions
Tottenham Hotspur

WATERLOO Despite the introduction of electrification into Waterloo some three decades or so earlier, ageing steam locomotives still managed to eke out their days shuttling to and from the station until the very last days of steam on the Southern Region. A case in point is No 30039, seen pulling an empty van train from the bowels of the station on 14 March. With a clear road and the job neither too onerous nor hurried, the driver leans casually on the cabside opening. Note the differing non-railway architectural styles in the background. The 'M7 Class' was built by Drummond for the L&SWR between 1896 and 1911 and all but two of the original 105 locos survived to work into Nationalisation in 1948. No 30039 was not surprisingly a Nine Elms engine in this view, but had previously served Salisbury, Plymouth (Friary), Fratton and Eastleigh among others. It was transferred to the Western Region on 30 January 1963, but was withdrawn nine days later without allocation to a specific shed.

WATERLOO We have seen No 30798 *Sir Hectimere* previously at Waterloo on p.5. Two months on from that view, the 'Round Table' member is still hard at work into and out of the terminus and is here about to leave with the same roster as on 16 March, the 2.54 p.m. semi-fast to Basingstoke. Some of the massive extent of Waterloo – at 21 it boasts the greatest number of platforms in the UK, handling well over 180million passengers each year – can be seen behind the train. Opening on 11 July 1848, it has seen numerous changes over its long life, not least the hosting and then losing the Eurostar services. Designed by William Tite, it was raised above marshy ground, on the south bank of the Thames, on a series of arches.

WATERLOO Looking across a few of the many platforms, No 34071 *601 Squadron* is doing its best to pollute this area of London before its sets off for the west in an evening rush-hour departure of 2 August. 601 (County of London) Squadron was formed at RAF Northolt on 14 October 1925, when a group of wealthy aristocratic young amateur aviators decided to form themselves into a Reserve Squadron of the RAF. Initially known as "the millionaires squadron", many of the affluent young pilots had little regard for the rigid discipline of the regular service, lining their uniform tunics with bright red silk and wearing blue ties rather than the regulation black. They played polo on brand-new Brough Superior motorcycles, drove fast sports cars and most owned their own private aircraft. However, the war quickly took its toll on the pre-war personnel and as replacements were drafted in the Squadron became as cosmopolitan as any other. No 34071 was a well-travelled engine, serving Ashford shed at this date; its end came on 14 September 1964, from Eastleigh.

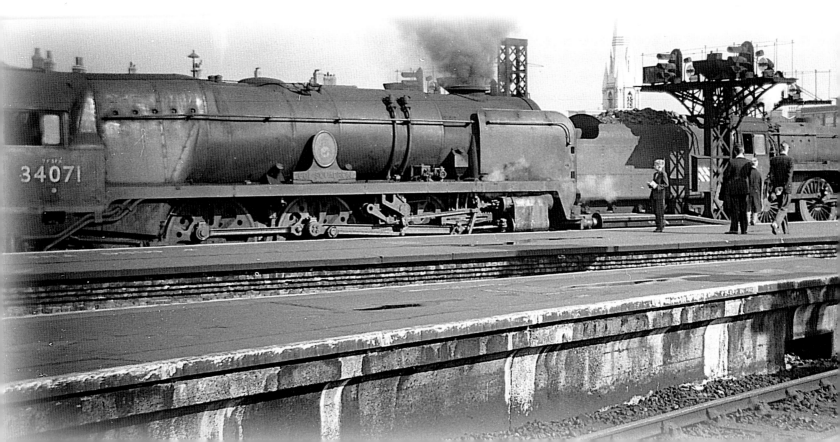

Right: **WATERLOO** Whilst the vast majority of steam locomotives operating out of Waterloo were ex-Southern Railway, even well into the days of British Railways, this situation began to change with the input of 'Standard' types from the mid-Fifties onwards. On 13 March, No 73082 *Camelot* takes the first steps away from the platform with a 3.54 p.m. departure.

Below: **WATERLOO** Another 'Standard Class 5', No 73084 *Tintagel*, sneaks up on its neighbour on 2 August, preparing to head west, as, left, No 30850 *Lord Nelson* patiently waits to leave with the Holland-American Boat Train express. Founded in 1873 as the 'Dutch-America Steamship Company', as a shipping and passenger line, operations changed over the years but the company survived into the 21st century, albeit within a greater Carnival Corporation.

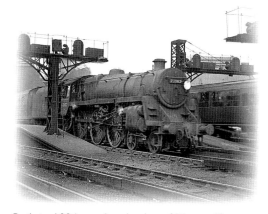

Built in 1926, as class leader of Maunsell's 4-cylinder 4-6-0s, No 30850 was later rebuilt with smokebox deflectors and double blast pipes, as seen here. An Eastleigh loco for its entire BR life, it was withdrawn on 24 September 1962 but, happily, was to be saved for preservation.

SALISBURY was one of those places, like Oxford and Banbury on the Western Region, Leicester on the Great Central and Grantham on the ECML, where trains paused to change locomotives. In common with the first three named, Salisbury saw visitors from other regions, as cross-region trains came into the area. To service these visitors – and the home stud that would take over – the engine shed grew to large proportions and even though 1961 was relatively late in the day, some of the size of the shed and the variety of motive power present can be seen on 10 June. From left to right are seen: No 5376, No 30502, No 73118 *King Leodegrance*, No 6841 *Marlas Grange*, No 34082 *615 Squadron*, No 34027 *Taw Valley*, No 7203, No 3212 and No 34031 *Torrington*. In addition, approximately 20 locos were resting inside the shed building. Initially provided with a shed facility in 1858, there were many changes over the years. The one seen here was new in 1901 and fulfilled its various functions until the end of steam on the Southern, on 9 July 1967. It then stood empty and progressively derelict for many years, before being demolished.

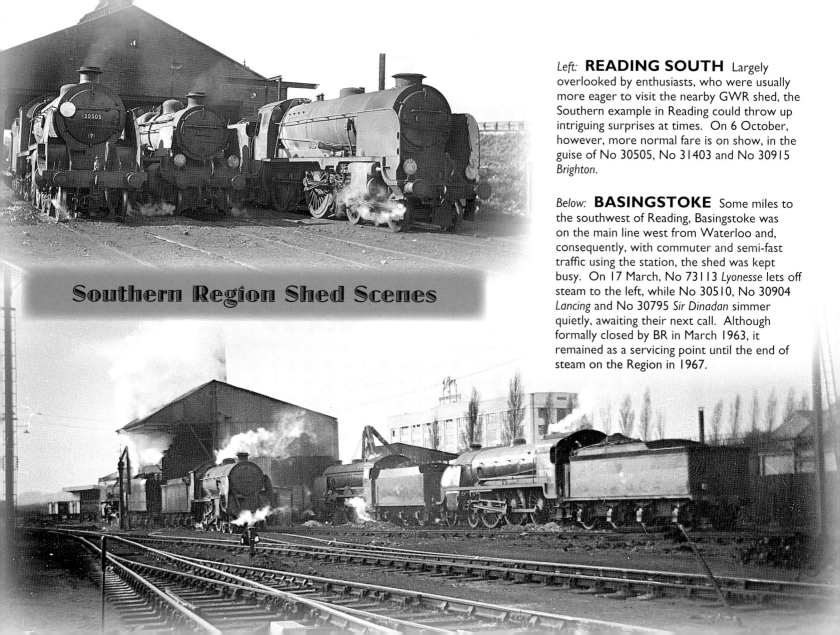

Southern Region Shed Scenes

Left: **READING SOUTH** Largely overlooked by enthusiasts, who were usually more eager to visit the nearby GWR shed, the Southern example in Reading could throw up intriguing surprises at times. On 6 October, however, more normal fare is on show, in the guise of No 30505, No 31403 and No 30915 *Brighton*.

Below: **BASINGSTOKE** Some miles to the southwest of Reading, Basingstoke was on the main line west from Waterloo and, consequently, with commuter and semi-fast traffic using the station, the shed was kept busy. On 17 March, No 73113 *Lyonesse* lets off steam to the left, while No 30510, No 30904 *Lancing* and No 30795 *Sir Dinadan* simmer quietly, awaiting their next call. Although formally closed by BR in March 1963, it remained as a servicing point until the end of steam on the Region in 1967.

Below: **BOURNEMOUTH** Moving towards the running line, No 30379 stands outside the main shed on the same day, with double-chimney 'Standard Class 4' 4-6-0 No 76065 behind. Note that both roads in view have pits, to take the ash and clinker from the hard worked locos. One of Drummond's large 'Class M7' 0-4-4Ts, No 30379 is here fitted with air pumps to enable it to operate push-pull services on local branch lines. Another well-travelled loco, its last shed was Three Bridges, from where it was withdrawn on 14 October 1963. The shed originally opening in July 1883, demolition, change and extension occurred over ensuing years, to accommodate changing traffic patterns, with the final layout surviving until the end of steam at Bournemouth from 9 July 1967.

Above: **BOURNEMOUTH** was another shed that saw changes of locos, but this time it was at the end of a route, rather than part way. Shoehorned into a cramped space immediately to the west of the station, it handled its task with distinction during its steam years, servicing, turning round and even repairing on occasions to keep the trains running. On 24 June, No 30824 stands outside the side shed, coaled, watered and turned on the turntable ready for its next run to London. The second of Maunsell's 'S15' express freight engines, built in 1927, it could often be seen on passenger duties. Working from Exmouth Junction, Salisbury (its shed when seen here), Basingstoke and Bricklayer's Arms sheds in BR days, it lost favour on 27 September 1965. It was reduced to scrap metal at Cashmore's yard, Newport just two months later.

Right: **GUILDFORD** A hot mid-summer's day – 1 p.m. on 21 June – casts a heat haze and somnolent air over Guildford shed, as seen from Farnham Road overbridge, nestling its half roundhouse alongside the cliff face. No loco numbers are given by the photographer, or are identifiable, but we are told that the shed that day included Classes N, U, C, G6, M7, B4, '700' and one of BR's diesel shunters (later to become 'Class 08'). Unique in the southern half of the country, the design of the shed was, like so many others around the UK, primarily dictated by topographical circumstances.

Left: **GUILDFORD** Turning through 180°, the view north from Farnham Road shows the station to the right and the coaling stage and servicing roads to the left of the running lines. At the same time of day and the same day as above, we are again denied loco numbers, but Classes include U, N, Q1, C2X and M7. The earliest shed was situated at the north end of the station, beyond the long covered footbridge visible above the station canopies, opening on 5 May 1845 and closing in 1887, when the position was required for the enlargement of the station. Note the piles of ash and clinker on the ground between the left-hand tracks, demonstrating why it became increasingly difficult in post-War years to recruit and retain staff.

Turning the Tables

Above: **READING SOUTH** Captured broadside, No 30505 stands on the turntable at this outpost of the Southern Region on 6 October, having brought freight from Feltham into the town. The original 'S15s' were designed by Urie and introduced in 1920. Envisaged as an express freight locomotive, the longer distances travelled on such duties led to some of them being endowed with eight-wheeled tenders from Drummond's era. No 30505 is one such, clearly visible in this view. A Bricklayer's Arms shed loco for the whole of its BR life, it was withdrawn on 19 November 1962, one of the earliest of the class to be dispensed with.

Right: **READING SOUTH** Another 'S15' that has brought freight to Reading on the same day as its 'sister' engine on p.16, No 30507 is here being manhandled on the turntable by the brute force of the fireman, on 6 October, as this shed did not possess a powered facility. Again with a Drummond eight-wheeled tender, '07' was another long-term resident of Bricklayer's Arms but, in this case, it survived until 6 January 1964. It's final journey was north, via the Midland Main Line, to George Cohen's scrap yard at Kettering in the following March. The first shed here was opened on 4 July 1849 but closed just three years later, replaced by one on the same site that lasted until 1875. The final one, seen here, opened in that year, on a site closer to the GWR main line and incorporating this turntable, enlarged to 65ft in Southern Railway days.

Left: **READING SOUTH** A view of the turntable from the other end on the same day. The occupant on this occasion is 'N Class' 2-6-0 No 31858, displaying its modified front end. Driver Warne and his mate pose from the cab for their portrait. Classified as 'mixed-traffic' locos by Maunsell, with 5'6" driving wheels, the final fifty of the class – including No 31858 – were built at Woolwich Arsenal and not acquired by the Southern Railway until 1925, eight years after the first of the class emerged from Works. This engine received new frames and a BR chimney just four months prior to this view, in June 1961 - last to be so converted . Serving Redhill, Hither Green and Guildford in BR days, the end came on 10 January 1966, being one of the last three of the 65-strong Class to remain in service.

Below: **GUILDFORD** Hey 'it's a dirty job but...' Somehow back then 'every boy wanted to be an engine driver when he grew up' or at least so we were led to believe! Judging by the level of ash around the pit and the subsequent state of the overalls even the 'Missus' is going to find train driving a dirty job!

The crew recharge the tanks of Adams 'Class G6' 0-6-0T No 30277 from one of Guildford shed's swan neck water columns. The class totalled 34 locos and they were built between 1894 and 1900. Having been taken into BR Southern Region stock, following nationalisation in 1948, No 30277 started her BR days based at Templecombe staying until 1951, she was transferred briefly to Basingstoke for 2 months, then drifted between Nine Elms, Guildford (twice) and Reading South. Her demise from service came on 8 December 1961.

To the left stands Drummond 'Class M7' 0-4-4T No 30378 which belonged to a class of 105 built between 1896 and 1911. Her BR days started at Eastleigh, to June 1959, then Guildford to April 1962, her steam finally ran out at Bournemouth on 7 January 1963.

Above: **SOUTHAMPTON DOCKS**
The date is 20 September and No 30071 is taking water....with one of the shed staff beating a hasty retreat from a potential bath! With duty code '9' on the front, '71' was one fourteen so-called 'USA' tanks, American 1942/43 built 0-6-0Ts acquired by the Southern Railway from the War Department in 1947. Purchased for use in Southampton Docks, they replaced older ex-SR types and did sterling work right through to their end in the mid-1960s, when they were replaced by diesels. Leaving the Docks for the glamour of nearby Eastleigh in June 1963, its record of service at the latter was to be impressive, with it lasting right up to the end of steam on the Southern Region on 9 July 1967.

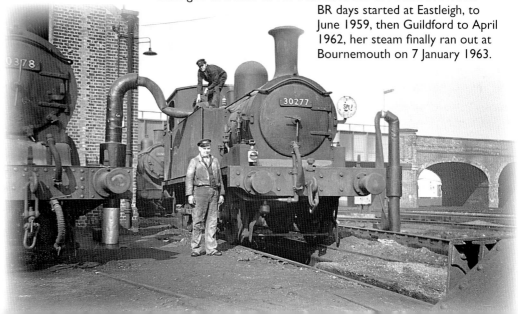

Around the Regions...

PETERBOROUGH Most ECML express trains to the north ran in a direct line from King's Cross station to Peterborough, but this one has taken a more circuitous route. Heading the 11.15 a.m. departure from London on 22 October, No 60015 *Quicksilver* has travelled via Cambridge, March and Peterborough East to arrive at the Great Northern station in the town and heralded the need for a water stop. The fireman looks after the business end of the water pipe to the tender, while the driver exchanges pleasantries with two trackside rail men. One of Gresley's famed 'A4' Pacifics, it emerged from Doncaster Works on 21 September 1935 as No 2510, the second of the class to be built. Its last Works visit was in May 1959, when the writing was on the wall for the class and it succumbed to the inevitable on 18 May 1963, from King's Cross shed.

Overleaf: **UFFCULME** Your authors make no excuse to readers of *Railways & Recollections 1961 Volume 1* for including this further shot of '1400' Class 0-4-2T No 1466 (formerly No 4866) at Uffculme. As we delve further and further into the Ray Ruffell archive we discover more and more gems! In line with many prolific photographers Ray it seems did not necessarily

print all the negatives from a roll of film. Having reproduced a platform end shot at the Hemyock terminus, as an inset on *page 13* in the first volume, from a print, we have now discovered further negatives of shots taken on the same day, 16 October, this being one of them.

There is so much detail in this shot that reflect the period that we have tried to reproduce the image as large as possible. No 1466 carries an 83C shed plate indicating that it is based at Tiverton Junction a sub shed to Exeter. Closer inspection reveals that Andrews & Miller are offering, 'Private Enterprise Housing', on a board affixed to the end of the wooden building to the left of the locomotive. Modellers will delight in the detail of the station building and the ornate gas lamp, the corrugated shed, wheelbarrow, oil drum and note the two metal milk crates, neatly interlocked one on top of the other each containing 'school sized' glass bottles, many readers will no doubt remember them. The branch passenger service regrettably ended on 9 September 1963, freight facilities here were lost in May 1967 except for private siding traffic and when the dairy at Hemyock closed on 31 October 1975 all traffic ceased and the line closed. The M5 motorway plans included an overbridge to accommodate the line but in the event although started on was rapidly filled in as the road opened after closure.

Below: **CAMBRIDGE** was more normally associated with express, semi-fast and branch line trains and the appropriate locomotives either shedded there or passing through. Whilst there were freight duties in the area, the sight of ex-WD 'Austerities' was not common. On 7 September, No 90514 (ex-WD No 79247) has worked into Cambridge on a goods turn and has repaired to the engine shed for refreshment and rest before the next outing. It had been a March resident for 3½ months in the middle of 1959, having migrated from Tilbury. An earlier home had been at New England (Peterborough) and subsequent moves would take it to Plaistow, Tilbury and New England again and then further north, to Retford, Colwick and, finally, Frodingham. Withdrawal was on 2 February 1966.

Above right: **CAMBRIDGE** A second view of Cambridge shed on 7 September, with a portrait of ex-LNER 'K3' No 61834, standing with No 90514 behind it. Another of Gresley's designs, the 'K3s' were built over a protracted time span, from 1924-37. With 5'8" driving wheels and 6ft boilers, they were truly a mixed traffic type, with a tractive effort of 30,030lb from the 72 ton locomotive. They were popular with crews and served their region well, not least through the War and on into Nationalisation. Eventually they were overtaken by changing traffic patterns and introduction on the Eastern Region of diesels, with the result that the last of the class was taken out of service in 1962. No 61834 left Cambridge a month after this view, on 7 October, to go to March, from where its end was on 9 June the following year; but the final 'K3' to work was probably No 61912, serving as a stationary boiler at New England shed until 1964.

1961 Arrivals & Departures

Births

Graham Macpherson (Suggs)	singer		13 January
Andy Taylor	singer		16 February
Laurel Clark	astronaut	(d. 2003)	10 March
Eddie Murphy	actor/comedian		3 April
George Lopez	actor/comedian		23 April
George Clooney	actor		6 May
George Alan O'Dowd (Boy George)	musician/producer		14 June
Kalpana Chawla	astronaut	(d. 2003)	1 July
Diana Spencer	Princess of Wales	(d. 1997)	1 July
Carl Lewis	athlete		1 July
William C McCool	astronaut	(d. 2003)	23 September

Deaths

Morris Stanley Nichols	English cricketer	(b. 1900)	26 January
George Formby	singer, actor/comedian	(b. 1904)	6 March
Thomas Beecham	composer	(b. 1879)	8 March
Gary Cooper	actor	(b. 1901)	13 May
Carl Jung	psychiatrist	(b. 1875)	6 June
Ernest Hemingway	author	(b. 1899)	2 July
Chico Marx	comedian	(b. 1887)	11 October
Earle Page	Australian PM	(b. 1880)	20 December

Right: **AVIEMORE** Stanier's version of a mix-traffic loco, built for the LMS, was his 'Black 5'. Built between 1934 and 1951 they had the luxury of later developments with steam and survived to very end of steam on 11 August 1968. Interestingly, at 72 tons (as with the 'K3') but with slightly larger driving wheels at 6ft, the 'Black 5s' had a noticeably lower tractive effort, at only 25,455lb, but they were able to work over any part of the LMS and, later, the BR system. Emerging in 1935, No 45179 is seen here at the head of a northbound mixed freight train, with the majority of vehicles conveying cement. A Scottish Region loco for the whole of its time with BR, it gradually moved south from Inverness, to Perth and on to the Glasgow area. Initially withdrawn on 19 January 1963 from Motherwell, it was re-instated on 16 February, only to be dispensed with again on the following 8 June.

CARDIFF   Cardiff's East Dock shed
(88B) have done a splendid job of cleaning on
their '5600' Class 0-6-2T No 6682 seen here
simmering at Cardiff Queen Street station.
Queen Street was and still is today considered
to be the central hub of the routes that radiate
from Cardiff providing interchange between
the London - Fishguard main line and the
various lines southwards to the coast and
northwards to the valleys.

The 200 Collett designed Class '5600'
locomotivess were built between 1924 and
1928 by the Great Western Railway at their
Swindon works or, in the case of the last
50 locomotives, for them, by Armstrong
Whitworth at their Scotswood Works in
Newcastle-Upon-Tyne. No 6682 was one of
the Newcastle built examples and was to run
for a further three years being withdrawn from
East Dock on 29 February 1964 from where
she was sent to Swindon Works for scrapping
in May of that year. Had she taken the much
shorter journey to Dai Woodham's yard in
Barry she might well have survived along with
no fewer than nine of the Class eight of which
were saved from Barry!

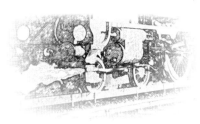

The driver of the 'Manor' leans on his cab cut-out and converses with the pipe-smoking gentleman in the overcoat, whilst the young boy, complete with grease top cap, seems more interested in the less glamorous loco behind. In the background, the FR train stretches from that Railway's Minffordd station and across the standard gauge line, with some of the AGM participants already on board. Others will follow, up the connecting footpath between the two stations from behind the lower platform building in the centre of the picture.

Note the standard to narrow gauge connection to the right, allowing coal traffic to come from the 'main line' to the FR. This facility was withdrawn sometime later in the decade. The FR's Minffordd station building – occupied by the Railway's General Manager in the 21st century – can be seen upper left. *Gerald Adams, MJS collection*

MINFFORDD The day may not have been the best, with rain dictating overcoats and umbrellas for some of the time, but this in no wise dampened the spirits of the travellers on the 'Festiniog Railway Special' of 22 April. In these still relatively early days of preservation of the FR – and with roads and cars still not conducive to fast and easy travel – the AGM's were considered sufficiently important occasions to warrant the organisation of a special train to bring interested parties to the Railway for the event. Often these would be hauled by two locomotives and the pairings were usually worth witnessing in their own right. For this year, the two are ex-GWR 4-6-0 No 7824 *Iford Manor* and 2-6-0 No 7310. The tour had run from Paddington-Ruabon behind No 6002 *King William IV* – thought to be the first 'King' to reach Ruabon – before handing over to the pairing seen here.

Mildenhall Signalbox

1961 TV Favourites a selection

Ask Mr. Pastry (BBC)
Childrens Sitcom starring Richard Hearne as Mr. Pastry & Dandy Nichols as Mrs Spindle

Comedy Playhouse (BBC)
The first of over 100 half hour sitcoms

Bootsie and Snudge (Granada)
A spin off from the *The Army Game* (BBC) featuring the demobbed characters played by Alfie Bass and Bill Fraser

The Morcambe and Wise Show (ATV)
The start of the legendary shows starring Eric and Ernie

The Rag Trade (BBC)
Fenner Fashions first hit the screen in 1961 starring Reg Varney, Peter Jones and Miriam Karlin and rapidly became a must see sitcom for thousands of viewers

The Avengers (ABC)
The detective series that starred Ian Hendry as *Dr. David Keel* and Patrick Macnee as *John Steed* in the first series and which went on to star Honor Blackman as *Cathy Gale* and Diana Rigg as *Emma Peel*

Coronation Street (Granada)
Should need no introduction, but having started in 1960 as a regional programme the legendary show went national in '61

MELTON MOWBRAY was on the LMS line from Leicester to Peterborough, via Oakham, but also had a connection south of the town towards Nottingham. This latter route was often taken by services that had travelled north from St Pancras but avoiding Leicester. On one such run, No 46133 *The*

Green Howards roars non-stop through Melton and past the loftily perched signalbox, with the 4.42 p.m. St Pancras-Sheffield express of 29 June. To the left are sidings serving the well known Petfoods factory. Rebuilt in July 1944 from the more antiquated, 'near-Claughton' original design, No 46133 was a well travelled

loco, shed-wise as well as operating distance, representing Leeds (Holbeck), London (Kentish Town) and Manchester (Trafford Park and Newton Heath). The end was on 23 February 1963 from the latter shed. *Frank Cassell, MJS collection*

MELTON MOWBRAY The station running-in board says it all, complete with the suffix 'Town', to differentiate the site from the ex-Great Northern station elsewhere in the town. Entering the station from the south, this train is running in the opposite direction to No 46133 on the previous page, but is also using the diversionary north-south route avoiding Leicester. On 26 April, No 45712 *Victory* slows for the station stop as the 6.20 p.m. Nottingham-St Pancras semi-fast service. The 'Jubilee', one of 191 built to Stanier's design between 1934 and 1936, was another locomotive that was used by many sheds, including, in its British Railways' days, the areas of Manchester, Derby and London. Its final home was Derby, until 30 November 1963. *Frank Cassell, MJS collection*

MELTON MOWBRAY The junction to Nottingham, referred to in the previous two pages, is here seen from the footplate of 'Austerity' No 90522, on southbound freight duties on 21 July. Appropriately named 'Melton Junction', the line to Nottingham strikes off to the right, with the 'main' line to Leicester going left and on which this train will pass. The former route closed to passengers on 6 June 1966, but into the 21st century, the junction has survived, as the link to the stretch to Widmerpool (closed on 28 February 1949 and roughly half way to Nottingham), via Old Dalby, where an important testing facility has been based. Virgin's 'Pendolinos' were tested on this route after it had been upgraded and electrified at the turn of the century. *Frank Cassell, MJS collection*

MELTON MOWBRAY Back in the station confines, we are now at the east end of the platform, to witness No 92058 lazily restarting its loaded coal wagons from a siding on the far side of the road overbridge on 26 April, after the passage of another passenger train. Note the rather untidy platform arrangement, left , leading to the barrow crossing. New in November 1955, to Heaton Mersey in Manchester, the 'Standard 9F' finally saw service at Carlisle (Kingmoor) shed, surviving to close to the end of steam on BR, being withdrawn on 2 December 1967.
Frank Cassell, MJS collection

1961
Happenings (1)

January
- The millionth Morris Minor produced
- Elsa the lioness made famous through Joy Adamson's book *Born Free* dies
- The Birth Control Pill sold in Britain's pharmacies for the first time
- *101 Dalmations* one of the all time classics from Walt Disney is released in the US

February
- Airliner crashes in Belgium all 18 members of the US World Figure Skating Team lose their lives
- Initial plans for London's Post Office Tower are released
- New York hit by blizzards - with over 16 inches of snow reported

March
- George Formby the popular singer, comedian and musician passed away
- Dr. Richard Beeching takes up his post as head of British Railways

April
- Yuri Gagarin of Russia becomes the first man in space
- Britain applies for membership of the European Economic Community
- Judy Garland returns after illness to perform at New York's Carnegie Hall to wide acclaim

Right: **LEOMINSTER** In its heyday, Leominster was blessed with an engine shed, tucked away to the east of the main running line, north of the station. The original facility had been to the south, but the one viewed here replaced that in 1901. As can be seen on 3 June, the two-road affair has a glazed, northlight pattern roof and gave respite for a small handful of locos – or wagons at this date! There was also a turntable, water column and coaling stage, required to deal with the needs of locomotives working the east-west branch from Leominster Junction (southwest of Worcester) to New Radnor, as well as the main Shrewsbury-Hereford line that ran through the station. The shed closed on 2 April 1962 and was fairly quickly demolished thereafter. Just two locomotives are present on this date. *Gerald Adams, MJS collection*

Left: **LEOMINSTER** The station was also notable for its lofty signalbox, perched above the bay platform. In this view from 3 June, the main line is to the right, a line that No 1445 will join shortly on its short run north to Tenbury Wells. Note that the signage here has lost its 'Change Here for Kington, New Radnor, Presteigne and Bromyard Line' following the withdrawal of some branch lines. The massive and precarious-looking signalbox replaced two smaller boxes south of the station when opened in 1901 and lasted until June 1964. *Gerald Adams, MJS collection*

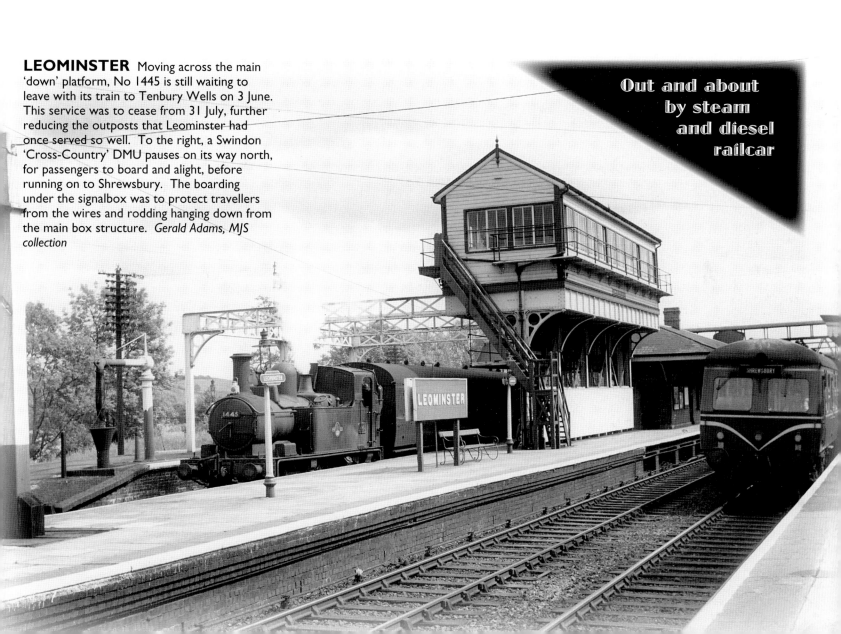

LEOMINSTER Moving across the main 'down' platform, No 1445 is still waiting to leave with its train to Tenbury Wells on 3 June. This service was to cease from 31 July, further reducing the outposts that Leominster had once served so well. To the right, a Swindon 'Cross-Country' DMU pauses on its way north, for passengers to board and alight, before running on to Shrewsbury. The boarding under the signalbox was to protect travellers from the wires and rodding hanging down from the main box structure. *Gerald Adams, MJS collection*

1961
Happenings (2)

May
- Alan Shepard becomes first American in space just a month after the Russians
- Formation of Coventry, Colchester and Canterbury Universities announced
- Gary Cooper the double *Oscar* winning actor dies of cancer
- George Blake found guilty of Spying and sentanced to 42 years in prison

June
- Dr. Michael Ramsey becomes the 100th Archbishop of Canterbury he will be the first Archbishop of Canterbury to visit Rome for an audience with the Pope
- Rudolf Nureyev defects in Paris while on tour with the Kirov Ballet Company

July
- British troops land in Kuwait due to the threat of invasion by Iraq
- Ernest Hemingway best selling author commits suicide

August
- Construction of the Berlin Wall starts, many East Germans flee to the West before the border is sealed
- The A6 murder committed - becomes the subject of long running appeal on behalf of James Hanratty against his conviction

with ex-GWR metals approaching from the opposite direction, striking southwest from Bewdley through Cleobury Mortimer. A small market town in Worcestershire, lying on the south bank of the River Teme, Tenbury Wells was renowned for over a century for its winter auctions of holly and mistletoe. Sadly, these ceased from 2007! Originally named "Temettebury", the "Wells" suffix was added following the discovery of mineral springs and wells in the town in the 1840s. *Gerald Adams, MJS collection*

Below: **WOOFFERTON JUNCTION** We are left in no doubt where we are now! Our redoubtable steed is at the confluence of the main line and branch, but will not now be running to Tenbury Wells, instead it will be travelling further up the main line, after crossing over to the nearside track, to reach Ludlow, some 4½ miles to the north. Once a busy junction station, Woofferton was graced at its height with a full range of goods facilities, including the ability to handle coal, minerals, furniture vans, motor cars, livestock and horse boxes, as well as passengers! Somewhat strangely, however, the goods yard did not possess a crane! *Gerald Adams, MJS collection*

Opposite page: **LUDLOW** Our tiny push-pull shuttle train has now travelled north from Leominster and briefly rests in Ludlow station, before running on to Shrewsbury and back again, on a complicated roster that included a trip to Tenbury Wells. Built by Collett for just this sort of work, No 1445 first appeared from Swindon Works in the mid-1930s, numbered No 4845. Renumbered sometime after 1946, No 1445 was predominantly a 'West Midlands/Borders' locomotive in its later years, serving Hereford, Banbury and Gloucester. The exception was a 26-month sojourn at Slough, from October 1961 to December 1963. Withdrawn in October 1964 it was scrapped at Birds Commercial Motors Ltd., Risca in March 1965. *Gerald Adams, MJS collection*

Above: **TENBURY WELLS** Still with our trusty 0-4-2T, we have reached the end of the run from Leominster on 3 June. At this date, the station was still technically a through route, with the short easterly branch from Woofferton forming an end-on junction

TENBURY WELLS A visit to the Tenbury Wells branch exactly three weeks later was to witness a change of motive power. On 24 June, ex-GWR railcar W23W comes to rest, having brought the summery party to the town, perhaps to taste the waters. Note the attractive and stoutly built station buildings, perhaps a little surprising, judging by the short length of platform that obviously was not expecting lengthy trains calling here! Working out of Newport (Ebbw Junction) when inherited by British Railways in 1948, its final home proved to be Worcester, from where

it had come on this day. Although one of the more 'modern' of the GWR railcars, it was to be affected by branch closures, such as this one the following month. It last saw service in 1964 and was cut up at Birds Commercial Motors Ltd. scrapyard, Risca in January 1965. *Gerald Adams, MJS collection*

1961
No 1 Records

January
I love you	*Cliff Richard*
Poetry in motion	*Johnny Tillotson*
Are you lonesome tonight	*Elvis Presley*

February
Sailor	*Petula Clarke*

March
Walk right back	*The Everly Brothers*
Wooden heart	*Elvis Presley*

April

Wooden heart - *stays at No 1*

May
Blue moon	*The Marcels*
On the rebound	*Floyd Cramer*
You're driving me crazy	*The Temperance Seven*

June
Surrender	*Elvis Presley*
Runaway	*Del Shannon*

July
Temptation	*The Everly Brothers*

August
Well I ask you	*Eden Kane*
You don't know	*Helen Shapiro*
Johnny remember me	*John Leyton*

September

Reach for the stars / Climb every mountain *Shirley Bassey*

October
Kon Tiki	*The Shadows*
Michael	*The Highwaymen*
Walkin' back to happiness	*Helen Shapiro*

November
His latest flame	*Elvis Presley*

December
Tower of strength	*Frankie Vaughan*
Moon River	*Danny Williams*

NEEN SOLLARS Traversing northeast from Tenbury Wells, along the ex-GWR branch towards Bewdley, we have reached Neen Sollars,. Much more of a wayside station than many on the branch, although again with decent sized buildings, designed by William Clarke and built in 1863. Happily, the building still stands into the 21st century, but without some of its more attractive features. Our single car train, formed of W23W on 24 June, pauses, perhaps to pick up the milk canisters, whilst the two locals watch the photographer. The eponymous village is situated close to the border with Worcestershire, has the River Rea flowing nearby and is south of the small market town of Cleobury Mortimer.
Gerald Adams, MJS collection

1961 Happenings (3)

September
- Sierra Leone admitted to the United Nations
- NASA announces that the new Lyndon B Johnson Space Centre would be established in Houston Texas

October
- The last steam hauled passenger train runs on the London Underground
- Malta gains independence from Britain
- The Ten Shilling note is reduced in size

November
- Stalingrad renamed Volgograd as part of Khrushchev's de-Stalinization policy
- Joseph Heller's *Catch 22* first published
- U Thant elected acting Secretary General of The United Nations

December
- First US troops land by helicopter in Vietnam signalling the start of the Vietnam war
- Israel finds Adolf Eichman guilty of crimes against humanity for his part in the Holocaust

Above: **WYRE FOREST** We have travelled further northeast and are now between Cleobury Mortimer and Bewdley. Again, just a single platform, with short platform, but impressive building. Named after the local forest that covers in excess of 6500 acres, freight handling facilities were withdrawn one week after this view of W23W on 24 June, with passenger services succumbing to the inevitable one year later, on 1 August 1962. Somewhat optimistically, the notice announces 'You may telephone from here'! *Gerald Adams, MJS collection*

CLEOBURY MORTIMER has been mentioned before. A junction between the GWR line from Bewdley to Woofferton Junction and The Cleobury Mortimer & Ditton Priors Railway branch to the latter named place, passenger services were withdrawn from the branch as early as September 1938, but freight ran on until 16 April 1965. In comparison, passengers lost their trains from the 'main line' in August 1962, before freight disappeared also on 16 April 1965. In this view from 24 June, our train of W23W prepares to leave the tiny station platform. *Gerald Adams, MJS collection*

BIRMINGHAM (NEW STREET) A view of New Street in happier times – for the enthusiast, with more interesting and greater variety of motive power and for the travellers, as the station is here not the 'black hole' that it has been for the past four decades! On 15 April, a smart looking 'Jubilee' No 45612 *Jamaica* lets off steam, next to 'Black 5' No 45447; whilst in the adjacent yard, a 'Standard Class 4' and a second (not so presentable) 'Jubilee' also let off steam as they wait for their next call. One of the 'Jubilees' named after countries in the Commonwealth, No 45612 was predominantly a Midland Main Line loco and presumably, therefore, allocated to Derby on this date, was here working a cross-country train, possibly from Derby to Bristol. Withdrawal was on 16 May 1964, from that shed. By comparison, No 45447 was a widely travelled engine but, apart from a five year stretch on the MML from 1954-59, was exclusively allocated to West Coast Main Line sheds. It survived until very close to the end of steam on BR, being taken out of service from Rose Grove on 13 July 1968. Although in excess of 40 million people pass through New Street station annually – making it the busiest station outside of London – it is, at the time of writing, not loved by many, gaining only 52% satisfaction rating in one survey. It was constructed as a joint station by the London and North Western Railway and the Midland Railway between 1846 and 1854 to replace several earlier unconnected rail termini, opening in 1851 as a temporary rail terminus of the London and Birmingham Railway. When completed, it had the largest iron and glass roof in the world, spanning a width of 212 feet (65 m) and being 840 feet (256 m) long.

Increasing usage and rail congestion led to various developments over the years before the roof suffered WWII bomb damage. From 1964 to 1966, the original station was demolished and the current 'hell hole' created, concurrent with electrification of the WCML, buried beneath various buildings, including a nine-storey office block. With yet more congestion, plans were drawn up in 2008 for a radical rebuilding that will, hopefully, greatly improve the travelling experience. *Gerald Adams, MJS collection*

Overleaf: **TYSELEY** Lying on the southern outskirts of Birmingham, Tyseley became an important junction for the GWR, being the parting of the ways for the line from Wolverhampton (Low Level) and Birmingham (Snow Hill), one striking southeast to eventually arrive at Paddington station and the other travelling broadly southwest towards Gloucester. Approaching the station on 29 July from the latter, otherwise known as the 'North Warwickshire Line', No 5014 *Goodrich Castle* wears a headcode that seems to indicate empty coaching stock. To the left, an up mixed train waits for the signals to clear the road. The adornment on the 'Castle's' smokebox is unidentified. *Gerald Adams, MJS collection*

Birmingham twixt Midland and Western...

TYSELEY The same location as the previous page, with the vantage point moved slightly to the photographer's left. Again on 29 July, another 'Castle', No 5018 *St Mawes Castle* approaches the station stop from the south, this time from the London route. A 'Hall' travels in the opposite direction. Built in 1932, No 5018 had long been a front-line express loco, but from 1950 onwards it saw more secondary duties, largely around the West Midlands, before a removal to Reading in 1958 and eventual withdrawal from there on 13 April 1964. *Gerald Adams, MJS collection*

Below: **ABERDEEN** The peg is 'off' and the driver of D5304 looks back to make sure there are no obstacles to him accelerating away from Aberdeen, with D5307, as an Edinburgh-bound express on 7 August. Beginning their working lives at Hornsey depot in late-1958, operating into and out of King's Cross, what became BR's 'Class 26' were transferred en-bloc to the ScR during 1960. These two went to Haymarket, east of Edinburgh, but were both eventually withdrawn from Inverness, in 1992 and 1977 respectively. D5304 was named *Spirit of Springburn* in May 1987; and D5307 was cut up at BR's Works in Glasgow in March 1978.

Right: **AVIEMORE** In steam days it was common practice to employ a locomotive as station pilot, at strategic places, either to avoid unnecessary delays in the event of a failure or to shunt local stock as required. Whilst often the culprit was a 'pensioned off' example of an older type, more modern power was also pressed into service as the needs dictated. On 17 August, still relatively new 'Standard Class 2' 2-6-0 No 78052 undertakes this duty. New in November 1955 to Motherwell, a move northeast came soon afterwards. By the time of its demise, from Bathgate on 29 February 1966, the eleven years three months life span was hardly a good return on BR's investment!

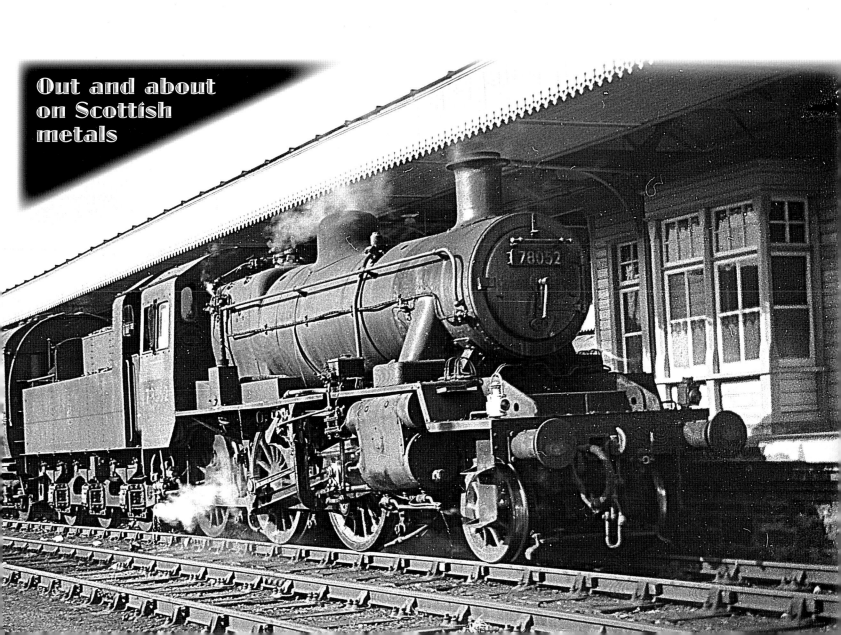

Left: **DYCE JUNCTION** Seen from a passing Inverness-Aberdeen diesel-hauled express, steam is fighting a rearguard action on 18 August, in the guise of 'B1' No 61350. Looking to be working hard, with an engineer's train of track panels, steam is obviously not prepared to go out without a fight! Another relatively new loco – to the ScR in August 1949, it lasted longer than many of its 'sisters', surviving until 26 November 1966.

Above: **THURSO** It is unlikely that the train is entering the station complex at such speed – even if it was late! – so one can assume that the photographer was deliberately attempting to create the illusion of great speed! D5323 enlivens the afternoon sunshine by its arrival from the south, at precisely 4.10 p.m., on 11 August.

SILLOTH The smiling face of BR! At Silloth station on 25 October, the driver and his mate grin from ear to ear as their portrait is taken, before they regain their positions in their train to take the travelling passengers on the 12.25 p.m. to Carlisle. This was reputedly the first branch line in Britain to have steam hauled passenger services replaced by DMUs as early as 1954. New to this line from Derby in December of that year, 'Derby Lightweight', diesel multiple unit No.79016, one of a type of unit destined for the more rural branch lines, just such as this, is seen here at the terminus.

Silloth was once a thriving railway centre with extensive yards to service the deep water port from where steamers to Scotland and Liverpool once operated. In 1856 The Carlisle and Silloth Bay Railway and Dock Company opened their line from Drumburgh to Silloth and utilised the Port Carlisle Railway Company's line from Port Carlisle to Carlisle via a junction at Drumburgh. Interestingly the section from Drumburgh to Port Carlisle then became horse drawn and was known locally as *The Dandy* - the carriage used survives as part of the national collection at York.

The North British Railway leased the line from The Carlisle and Silloth Bay Railway and Dock Company in 1862, absorbing it completely in 1880. The line passed into LNER ownership in the 1923 grouping and British Railways on Nationalisation in 1948. The line succumbed just short of 3 years after this shot was taken on 7 September 1964 As for No 79016 this unit was destined for the scrapyard being cut at Arnott Young's yard in Troon in June 1969.

Index

EARDLEY YARD Driver Ackehurst and his fireman stand with Pilot Driver (from Clapham Junction to Eardley), enjoying a brief rest break after arriving with empty stock from Walton-on-Thames on 4 October, before they climb back up onto No 33014 and make their return journey. The chalk message on the tender proclaims 'Prepared don't take tools 22/9'!